HOME
Safe
HOME

T0011978

HOME Safe HOME

DON'T BE AN EASY TARGET

SCOTT LILLY

TATE PUBLISHING
AND **ENTERPRISES**, LLC

Published by Tate Publishing & Enterprises, LLC
127 E. Trade Center Terrace | Mustang, Oklahoma 73064 USA
1.888.361.9473 | www.tatepublishing.com

Tate Publishing is committed to excellence in the publishing industry. The company reflects the philosophy established by the founders, based on Psalm 68:11,
"The Lord gave the word and great was the company of those who published it."

Book design copyright © 2016 by Tate Publishing, LLC. All rights reserved.
Cover design by Albert Ceasar Compay
Interior design by Gram Telen

Published in the United States of America

ISBN: 978-1-68333-117-9
1. Self-Help / General
2. Reference / General
16.06.06

To the men and women of public safety. Also to those who lost their lives or have been seriously injured in the line of duty. Every day, their lives are put on the line for a low-paying, thankless job, which takes them away from their families, sometimes never to return. Because of the dedication, commitment, and love for the job, they do it every day, without hesitation. Swearing to an oath to protect and serve, placing them in harm's way to make our communities a safer place.

Contents

Preface

Using my law enforcement experience of over twenty-one years, I thought of another way to combat crime or catch it before it happens, providing home and business owner's information, making them aware of certain crimes as well as steps to prevent them. This is also known as a suppression tactic.

Many victims of crimes have told me, "You know, I meant to do that, just never got around to it." By this time, meeting with an investigator means it's already too late. They are now being added as a crime statistic, and I can only hope it is due to the loss of property and not something more serious. However, in some cases, this does occur.

I wanted to share my experience so individuals can reduce their chances of becoming a victim of crime. When a crime is committed against you, especially in your home, you lose your sense of security, and the feeling of being violated sets in. This violation affects you and other members of your family, to include your children—the feeling of knowing someone else was in your home and your property was taken.

Once this happens, it is hard to restore what has been taken from you. I have included many helpful suggestions, hints, and tips that can be used in your home, business, or just simple day-to-day activity. Our homes are considered our sanctuary and safe havens from everyday life. Don't put off making needed improvements to protect you and your family.

Introduction

Many years ago, the world was a better place and people were different. Most lived in neighborhoods where you could leave your doors unlocked, your windows open. You might have even left your keys in the ignition, without worrying if your car would be there the next morning when you walked out to leave for work.

You and your neighbor would borrow tools from one another, making sure they were always returned. Trust went a long way, and the verbal agreement, followed by a handshake, was as good as signing your name on the dotted line. Trusting others was much easier and safer back then.

You didn't worry about your neighbors, and most knew each other by first names. You watched each other's children or spent time cooking out and playing together. When you walked outside and didn't see your kids, you did not get alarmed. You knew they were at the neighbor's house playing or at the park. Back then, people were not as alarmed about everything as they are today.

Crime has always been a part of everyday life. But years ago, there wasn't as much news coverage as there is today. Crime was much less during those times, and the criminal justice system was much harder. Punishment actually meant time in prison without credit for days you don't actually serve.

Criminals feared being sent to the "chain gang" as they called it, and knew if they got ten years, they would serve the majority of their time. They were not given cable TV and the amenities prisoners receive today. Criminals do not fear the justice system because of early release and the ease of doing time, instead of the hard labor as it was in the past.

Because of the system that fails, we have criminals back on the street—criminals who shouldn't be back on the streets doing crimes they were locked up for to begin with. Only a very small percentage learns from serving time and makes an honest attempt at being an active member of society when released.

The other percentages of criminals, who are housed with older, more experienced criminals, sit around for hours and talk about new ways to commit crime—without getting caught. Once back on the street, they can't wait to test newfound skills to see if they work.

Because of the prison systems being very overcrowded, with thousands coming in every day, many are released to make room for others. This means drug dealers, thieves, thugs, burglars, and sex offenders are released, being put on probation or parole, to make room in the system.

Statistics show those released early on probation or parole will violate the conditions within the first six months of being released. Some abide by the rules and report as ordered by the court system. Others will usually violate within the first forty-eight to seventy-two hours of being released. They will resort back to crime and immediately look for old friends, local drug dealers, or known criminal element.

During my career, I have dealt with repeat offenders on many occasions. I have also found myself dealing with the children of parents I arrested ten to fifteen years ago. This indicates to me in some cases there is a cycle that repeats itself with each generation.

Don't get me wrong, not all of those children turn out bad; some learn from the mistakes of their parents and choose a different path. The reason for this is they want a better life for themselves or their children. They choose to become a member of society rather than an outcast, as their parents were.

The money criminals make from their crimes usually isn't spent to support families or raise the children, as most would like to believe. Greed and addiction are the two leading causes of crime, addiction being where most proceeds go to. Through many years of speaking to suspects and conducting interviews, I can honestly say I never had one tell me they committed crimes to support or feed the family.

The purpose for this book is to share with you the things I have learned over the years and help reduce your chances of becoming a victim of crime. As you will notice, I said reduce your chances, not eliminate. There is no guarantee you will not become a victim of crime. But making yourself less of an easy target greatly reduces your chances of becoming a victim.

1

About the Criminals /
Insight into a Criminal's Mind

People often ask why criminals don't just go out and get a job. This question has many answers, but most likely they don't want one or are too lazy to get one. The other reason: most have an addiction to illegal narcotics, and because of this, passing a drug screen is somewhat impossible.

The other reason I find, a lot of criminals complain they can't find a job because of their criminal history and no one will hire them. In some cases this may be true, but some of them wouldn't hold down a job if they did become employed.

Victims have asked why their house? Were they being watched or targeted for some specific reason? Most likely the answer to this question is no. Most criminals target a specific area or a specific type of residence, not people. They look for secluded houses or homes that appear the easiest to break into, reducing the chances of them getting caught.

Criminals will drive around looking for a specific type of home or location before committing a crime. This sometimes helps law enforcement in connecting criminals to a rash of crimes because of the M/O or specific things they normally do when committing crimes.

When investigating crimes, I use one technique that proved successful in many circumstances. I would ask the victim to clear their mind. Then when I ask the question, I told them not to think about it and say the first thing that comes to mind. The question I would ask is "Who do you think did this?"

A large percent of the time, the victim would say a name within a few seconds. Most of the time looking further into this person, I found they either committed the crime or had some involvement in it. This made recovering property easier, and most times when confronted, the suspects would admit to the crime.

Many of us have members of our families or friends who are addicted to some type of illegal drugs. Or they may be going through some type of hardship, which made them feel like this was a necessary evil at the time. Either way, when deciding prosecution, consideration should be given to whether or not they will do it again if not prosecuted. If illegal drugs are the reason, most likely they will go back, and the addiction should be addressed immediately with some type of intervention.

2

Ensuring Home Safety

Let's start simple. If you are in the market for a new home, you want to protect your investment. As you are looking at your new home and think you found one, let's find out about the neighborhood or area we are moving to. If you are already a home owner but need to reevaluate security, following some simple steps will reduce your chances of becoming a victim of crime.

But you say the real estate agent told you "This was a nice neighborhood with great schools." Well, I am not going to say they would "stretch the truth" just to get a commission check, but *honesty is not always the best policy*. This is especially true if you want to make money in the real estate market with today's economy.

The way to reassure yourself you are moving somewhere you want to move your family, contact the local law enforcement agencies in that area. If you mention your neighborhood and they start laughing, this could be a clue! The officers work the streets and know the people as well as the crimes and criminals. If it is a bad neighborhood, you can bet they will give you a straight answer.

Technology has enabled us to do many things for ourselves that we once had to depend on others for or pay them to do for us. Almost everyone has access to the Internet, and if you don't, most of your local libraries offer it, some for free. This tool provides many answers to simple questions.

There are many sites you can go to investigate the area you are moving into. One thing in particular I like to mention is if you have children or will be living alone; check with your local law enforcement websites. These offer names and addresses of registered sex offenders as well as known criminals who may live in your area.

Okay, you have found a home, and it's actually in a good area. My question: does that make you safe from crime? The answer is most definitely not. You as the new homeowner must make simple adjustments to not eliminate but reduce your chances of becoming a victim. Always remember that the smallest investment into your home could mean the difference between being and not being victimized.

The first place to start is look at your door and window locks. Most homes nowadays are built with a door lock and also a dead bolt. If you don't have both on every door, that should be your first project. You can do this yourself, but if you are like me and not much of a handyman, it sometimes pays to have a professional install them.

Talk with your new neighbors, and usually one of them will know someone who will not only do a good job but maybe save you some money in the process. There are usually local listings in the phone book on individuals who offer these types of small repairs. Shop around and get the best price.

There are several websites dedicated to this type of information that offer names and information as well as customer reviews on local businesses for these types of repairs. This way you will have some idea of prices, quality of repair and what others felt about the work done. Two of those websites is www.angieslist.com and www.homeadvisor.com.

While looking at your door locks, I also suggest looking at the mounting screws for locks or dead bolts. These are usually about two inches long and thin. Depending on the type of door frame you have, try using longer, thicker screws. This reinforces the locking mechanism, making it a little harder to kick in.

There are several types of dead bolts that are with or without a key. There are good and bad with both. If you have a keyless dead bolt, someone can break a window, reach through, and open the door. This can't be done with the key dead bolt; however, if the criminals want in bad enough, they may just break the door down to gain entry.

The other issue with key entry is if during a fire or emergency at your home, you have to unlock the door. If the key gets lost in the panic, you now have a separate issue. I suggest talking with a home builder or your local hardware store for what best suits your needs. Everyone is different, and therefore this decision would be left up to the homeowner.

Window locks are just as important as the door locks. Make sure your windows have adequate locks on them. If looking at your window locks from the outside, push hard on the window inward. If the locking mechanism slides out from under the lock part, consider having them changed.

The best type of windows that offers a good source of security is the double slider window. You must first raise the inside window to access the outside window. Once you have accessed the outside window, you must slide two locks at the bottom of the window, inward, before it can be raised. There are security notches cut into the window frame that prevent these spring-type locks to bypass the notches.

You have the initial lock on the inside window, which is minor. The slide notch locks on the outside window offer much more security, and I would imagine the only way this window could be entered is by breaking the window. I am not sure who manufactures these types of windows, but I am sure Home Depot, Lowe's, or any builder could provide a brand name.

Another thing I suggest is to take an old broom or mop handle and cut it to the length of the top sliding portion of the window, in the upright position. Place the wedge in the window so that it can't be raised until the stick is removed. This also works well for sliding glass doors.

Hardware stores such as Home Depot, Lowe's, Ace and a few others sell round sticks of wood. You can purchase a long piece, which would be sufficient to do several windows with. Make sure the size of the wood is thick enough to sustain pressure and doesn't snap. Depending on the number of ground-level windows you have, this shouldn't be too costly.

Keep in mind if you use a window-unit AC, this is another method or point of entry. As suggested above, cut a stick to the length of the window above the unit to prevent the window from being raised to remove it. Another option is to connect the unit permanently to the window with screws.

Hardware stores, especially your larger ones, carry a vast array of reinforced door and window locks. They also have employees who can show you what works best and what doesn't. You will need to know the type of doors and windows you have as well as the measurements. Oftentimes, taking a picture with you will help make the right choice.

3

Alarm System

I have been asked many times about getting an alarm system. My response is always the same: yes, you should. Having an alarm system in your home is never a bad thing. When you weigh the pros and cons of having one, the pros always win. If you can afford it financially, then I say yes, have one.

Many years ago alarm system companies were few and far between. Nowadays, you have numerous companies fighting for your business and special offers of "free installation," which is very hard to beat. Just keep in mind the old saying, "You get what you pay for." Have the salesperson tell you the number of sensors you will receive with the free installation. I also suggest asking about accessories like an extra keypad or keychain remote.

If you can get a great alarm system, with free installation, consider that a bonus. When it comes to the security of your home, cost should not be an issue; but in that same aspect, don't overstep your financial boundaries.

Let me say this to the naive people of the world. Just because you have an alarm system *does not* mean that your home will not get broken into. It does, however, reduce your chances of getting broken into. The other thing I suggest is put up all the alarm company signs you can, letting the criminals know you do have one.

Some but not all criminals pay attention to alarm signs. If they see a home or business posted with an alarm sign, they will most likely move on to the next one. They know these systems are monitored, and as soon as entry is made and the alarm goes off, they know police are on the way, who is someone criminals are not eager to see.

Others ask about the use of surveillance video systems, and again, I say if you can do it financially, then it's added protection. Video systems can be rather costly and complicated. I suggest and urge business owners to have them but tend to suggest other means of security to homeowners.

Again, this depends on the homeowner who bears the cost of installation. But in the event your home is broken into, you have visual proof, which can assist in the identification of suspects and prosecution. Suspects, as well as defense attorneys, hate video footage of crimes, and it's responsible for many plea deals in the past.

This again goes without saying that you get what you pay for, so unless you are willing to pay for a good system, you may find that you are throwing away money that could be used for other things. While searching for a home video surveillance system, do plenty of shopping. Look for the best cameras and installation, at the lowest price. Make sure the IRs (infrared lights) in the cameras are good enough to illuminate the suspect and the area. IR lights can't be seen by the naked eye but will light up an area at night undetected.

Video surveillance systems are much more available these days. Use of nanny cams and small video camera systems may be ideal to suit your needs and some will even allow you to monitor them from your cell phone. Most are less expensive and can be purchased at stores such as Best Buy. These can usually be installed very easily.

Whether you get an alarm system, video surveillance system, or both, find out the areas they cover. If you see an area that isn't covered, speak up and let the installer know. Make sure the alarm or video covers key areas and especially the areas most secluded, as these are key points of entry.

I also suggest the use of alarm, video, dummy cameras and Beware of Dog signs. Why? you might ask. If a criminal is about to break in and see a camera, they don't know if it works or not. They may leave or just cover their face, so this may or may not work. The alarm or video surveillance sign is another. They don't know if you do or don't have these systems. The dog sign may give them a second thought about climbing the fence. These signs are available online or at many local hardware stores.

4

Firearms

Home- or business owners, ask if they should purchase a firearm. I am an advocate of personal protection; however, the purchase of a firearm depends on the person buying. If you are someone who doesn't know much about firearms or have never owned one, then this should be given careful consideration before making the purchase.

If you have never owned or shot a firearm, you should become familiar with the firearm. Make sure to get adequate training or instruction before trying to protect yourself and your home. Always remember that once a bullet leaves a gun, you can't take it back; and as the firearm owner, you are responsible for its use and safety.

Always keep your firearms in a safe place and away from children. There are numerous firearms accidents each and every year. These unnecessary accidents take a life or seriously injure children who are playing with firearms. Free gun locks are available from some local law enforcement agencies and are very simple to use.

There are other types of personal protection equipment available, such as pepper spray, stun guns and Tasers. Please remember, whatever the equipment or weapon, without adequate training, they can be taken and used against you. Even after receiving training, I suggest practicing to better prepare you if the use of this equipment is needed.

5

What to Do in Case of Burglaries

Having responded to many residential and commercial burglaries over the years, I have one suggestion that will help the owner as well as law enforcement. If you come home or arrive to your place of business and find it has been broken into, *do not* go inside. Get back into your vehicle, lock the doors, and call 911. Wait until law enforcement arrives and clears the home or office.

Remember, this is a crime scene, and entering could disturb valuable evidence that could be used to catch those responsible. Law enforcement understands this is your home or office. Law enforcement understands you have been violated and this is a stressful time for you. Try and remain calm and remember they are there to help you. You must also keep in mind, if they are going to do the investigation correctly, nothing needs to be disturbed until the officer tells you it is clear for you to enter.

Something as simple as walking inside can disturb fingerprints, footprints, fibers, clothing, blood or other types of DNA. This is the evidence that can be used to locate suspects or assist in prosecution. Once you enter, after being told to do so, try not to touch or move things without notifying the officer first. *This is very important.*

6

Lighting (for Both Business and Homes)

Outside lighting is very important around your home or business. Darkness provides cover and concealment for criminals, which they will use to their advantage. Your home doesn't have to look like an airport at night, but adequate lighting in well-placed areas is ideal for making you less of an easy target for criminals.

Some career criminals might actually do surveillance on a home before entering it. If they do, they may catch on to a motion sensor light and realize no one is at home, so use caution if using these. Flood lights or other outside lights wired into your home's electrical system usually work best for security purposes. Light timers can also be a good source of security, but these too can be figured out if the criminal is that dedicated.

7

Reporting Bad Guys

If at any time you are at home and hear something or see someone outside on your property, call 911. Do not go outside and confront or make contact with the person. You have no knowledge of this person or if they are armed. You also have no knowledge of what their intentions may be. Allow law enforcement to respond, make contact, and find out why the person is there. If you see a vehicle, safely try and obtain a tag number, vehicle description, as well as the number of occupants. Try and look at distinct things that would help better identify the person or vehicle.

A very common thing among burglars is to drive up to a home and knock on the door. If someone answers, they will ask if some person lives there, who most likely does not. If no one answers, this is when they will make their move. If you are at home and this happens, as soon as the person leaves, call 911. Get a description of the car, tag if possible, description of occupants, and direction of travel.

This may assist law enforcement in locating the vehicle. Most times this will occur between 7:00 a.m. and 4:00 p.m., when most people are at work. Even though you were at home, others may not have been, and it is likely their homes were broken into.

There will be a record of your call into dispatch. If it's discovered other homes in the area were broken into, then your call may be the break in the case. Investigators will look up this information, and if your information is found, the investigator will follow up on it. This information may lead him to the bad guy, or at least give him a direction to start.

8

Gates, Fences, Doors (for Homes, Businesses, and Cars)

We all strive to make our homes look the very best both inside and out. Sometimes, however, the very thing we look at as beauty or an improvement is looked at by others as cover and concealment. Privacy fences are great for privacy; however, they should lock from the inside. If you do have a privacy fence, make sure it is locked as this provides criminals the perfect working environment to gain entry into your home unseen.

Most "normal people" do not think like criminals. This is why when landscaping their home, they don't give thought to putting shrubs and trees in certain areas. Criminals look for things like this to make concealing themselves easier to gain entry into your home or business.

When landscaping your yard with shrubs or trees, especially around windows or doors, find out exactly what size they will be. If they will cover the windows or provide a hiding place next to your window, you may want to consider another type to place in this area. Remember, if they have concealment, they can work getting into your home or business unseen.

Using the same thought process on size, I also suggest, around doors and garage doors, using smaller shrubs or trees. If you can walk behind the shrub or tree and conceal yourself, then so can a criminal. When we exit our vehicle to go inside our home, we are usually looking for keys or thinking of something else. This makes us vulnerable to attack at these locations.

If you have automatic garage doors, wait until you have a visual on the door before opening it. Keep watching it until you pull into your garage, which prevents someone from sneaking in. Putting large shrubs next to your garage doors can be used as concealment. Once inside your garage, close the door before getting out, if feasible.

If you are able to see your front door or garage door and the areas around these doors, then you are less likely to be attacked at this location. Prior to exiting your vehicle, look around and make sure everything appears normal. If you see your door open or something that doesn't look right, stay in your car with the doors locked, drive to a safe location, and call 911.

9

Spare Keys

Hiding spare keys for guest and family members is not usually a good idea. Most buy decorative types of key hiders, which are usually very easy to spot. If the need arises for a spare key, following some of the following suggestions works better. Some criminals take the time to look for spare keys, which is why using them isn't a good idea.

The suggestions I have often made to individuals expecting family members or guest: make arrangements ahead of time to get them a key. If you are not able to do this, leave the key with a trusted neighbor or another family member who could meet your guest at the home with the key.

Be very cautious as to who has knowledge of a spare key and its location. Advise children who come home from school with friends of not allowing them to know where the key is. This information may be used by the friend or told to someone else who may use this information to get into your home.

10

Items Inside the Home

Let's talk for a minute about the property you have in your homes. Each of these items has a monetary or sentimental value. As we all know, sentimental value can't be replaced. Criminals do not care about sentimental value; all they are concerned about is the monetary value. So I urge you to take a few simple steps to further protect each of these.

I would feel comfortable saying that at least 90 percent of the world does not take the time to record serial numbers of property in their homes. Most property has a manufacturer's serial number on it that makes it unique. It is very important to write these numbers down and keep them in a safe place.

Items that have serial numbers are electronics, firearms, tools, ATVs, lawn mowers, weed eaters, toys, gaming systems, cameras, iPods, cell phones, computers, printers, watches, appliances (washer, dryer, stove, microwave), and many other items. If something in your home has a serial number, write it down.

If you work in the construction, landscaping, or other outdoor trade, which requires you to leave your tools outside, then keeping these serial numbers is especially important.

When on job sites, you can't stay with your tools, and them getting gone happens more easily. Take a moment to log these numbers on the tools you use on a regular basis.

Things such as utility or enclosed trailers, boat and watercraft trailers, campers, or anything made to pull behind a vehicle should be equipped with a trailer lock. These come in all shapes and sizes and are fairly inexpensive. Utility trailers are very easy to tow away and easy to convert to being untraceable. Protect your investment with a trailer lock and record all serial numbers.

Now, for those items that don't have a serial number and is large enough to be engraved somewhere, do just that. You can go to Home Depot, Lowe's, or any place that sells tools and purchase a small engraver. When engraving something, always remember to put it in a place that only you would know to look. This can be used for identification if the police recover your property.

My favorite is the Dremel Tool. It has many uses, and one of those is as engraving tool. This can be used to inscribe your initials, the last four digits of your SSN , your birthday, or something unique that only you would recognize. You can do this on anything that does not have a serial number.

You ask why these numbers are important to have. First, it identifies it as your property and is the only thing that will help recover it if it is stolen. Second, if you have these numbers when the initial police reports are taken, the officer can take that number and enter it on the National Crime Information Computer system.

If an officer in any jurisdiction has contact with your property and runs the serial number through NCIC, it will return stolen from the agency that entered it. This will provide the recovering officer with date of theft, the agency who filed the report, and the agency case number. This agency will seize the property, which will be returned to you or the insurance company if a claim has been paid.

You ask, "What if the serial number has been removed?" Well, in most states, it is illegal to remove or alter the serial number of any item. It is also illegal to be in possession of any item that does not have a serial number, which generally comes with one from the manufacturer. Mere possession of these items can result in the arrest of the person having them.

Items such as collectibles, valuables, and guns should be kept in a safe or a safety deposit box. Many of these items can't be replaced if stolen, and insurance companies are not likely to give you the value of what the item is actually worth. If it has sentimental value, go that extra step to ensure it stays in your family as intended.

The price of gold per ounce at the current time is very high. If you will look around your local shopping areas, you will see "We buy gold" stores popping up all over the place. Thieves are now stealing, as always, gold jewelry, which are then sold to one of these stores or local pawnshops. The stolen jewelry is usually sent off and melted within ten days of being stolen.

Some states regulate stores such as "We buy gold" stores, pawnshops, and recycling places for metals through the precious metals law. However, it does not prevent them from purchasing stolen jewelry, which is very hard to identify. However, these businesses are subject to criminal laws if knowingly caught purchasing stolen jewelry or metals.

As a property owner for jewelry, I often suggest taking photographs of the jewelry and keeping a list of each specific piece as well as the value of this particular piece. If in the event your jewelry is stolen, law enforcement can use your photos to take to local shops to see if your items have been purchased by them. This can also be used for insurance purposes as well.

If your items are located in a pawnshop, there are procedures that are taken by law enforcement to recover your property. These procedures are also used to assist the pawnshop in recovering the money they lost, through prosecution of the suspects who sold the property to them. If you as an individual find an item stolen from you in a pawnshop, contact your local law enforcement.

Just like jewelry, many of the items stolen—whether it's from inside your home, garage, storage building, and vehicle—may very well end up in one of your local pawnshops or somewhere else. These items can be tools, chain saws, lawn mowers, weed eaters, trimmers, leaf blowers, or any other item left unattended.

During the spring or summertime, when you are working on your yard, it is never a good idea to leave these items lying around, especially if you live close to the roadway. Most of these items, except for the lawn mower, can be stolen in less than a minute, and without a serial number, recovering them is unlikely. Depending on if you have a riding or push mower, these too can be stolen rather quickly, sometimes less than five minutes.

For those of you who have boat docks, remember: never store anything of value on the boat or boathouse. There has been an increase of waterfront crimes over the years due to ease of doing the crime unseen. This is also true if you live in a cove, which increases the chances. Make sure any valuables are locked up or secured in your residence or storage area.

Items such as fishing poles, skis, wakeboards, tubes, depth finders, and GPS devices should be secured in another location. Criminals are getting more and more creative, going to new lengths to commit crimes. This is one of them.

11

Mailboxes

Most of what I have talked about so far deals mainly with property crimes in relation to your home. One thing most homeowners do not think about is the mailbox at the end of your driveway. More problems and crime comes from this little box than you can imagine.

Working as a patrol officer, I would say my number one complaint for homes is trying to find them. Your street numbers are *very important*. They should be displayed visible and large enough to be seen. During an emergency, time is very important, and if your home can't be located, it takes away precious time. This time could be better used in dealing with the emergency at hand.

Home Depot, Lowes, Walmart, Ace, and other hardware stores sell accessories for mailboxes. Numbers should be large and reflective if possible. There are also solar-powered address lights available, which illuminate your street numbers. Whatever you choose, this should always be a priority. If they can't find your address, they can't find you.

If you live off the roadway and share a driveway with other homes, place a sign in your yard that shows your correct address. Display the numbers where they can be seen from a distance, especially at night. This prevents your home from being passed, where law enforcement or fire personnel would have to turn around to come back.

The other crime is criminals who drive around on rural roads, subdivisions, and city streets. They are looking for mailboxes with the red flag lifted, which draws attention to it. Criminals know this is most likely a check that is being mailed to pay a bill. Criminals will steal your mail without your knowledge.

Criminals will then take and do what is known as washing or bleaching the check. This is done with common chemicals that remove the ink and make it a blank check. Criminals then write the check for a different amount and cash it. You will not know until you review your bank statement.

The easy way to avoid this situation is by *never* mailing a check from your home mailbox. If you are mailing bills, always take them to the post office and place them in the mail there. If you have elderly family members who are known to mail out bills from home, help them avoid this by dropping the mail off for them.

If you have an elderly family member who receives some type of check on a monthly basis, such as Social Security or a retirement check, contact the check distributor and look into direct deposit. This reduces the chances of a check being stolen from mailboxes and also prevents the need of going to the bank.

12

Ensuring Safety of the Elderly in the Family

While speaking about elderly family members, if you see a change in their behavior, find out why. It may be for medical reasons or they may have been the victim of a scam and or another type of crime. They may not want others to know because of the embarrassment. Elderly victims will oftentimes not report a crime that has happened, but tell family members instead. If you are that family member, contact law enforcement and report the crime.

Sometimes dementia and Alzheimer's causes actions that are not normal. If you have a parent or other elderly family members who wanders off, look at other means of keeping them safe. Have a neighbor check on them regularly or check into a wrist-type GPS locator; in case they get lost, they can be quickly found. These types of locators are available from several different companies online.

I would like to also mention family members that sometimes keep large amounts of cash, in their homes. This is not solely for elderly, but for anyone who does this—maybe a self-employed individual. It is never a good idea to keep large amounts of cash at home, or even if traveling. It's nice to always have emergency cash, but keep it to a limit, such as $100 or $200. Be very cautious as to who has knowledge of this, as it can attract home invasions and burglaries.

Identity theft and credit card fraud is one of the nation's biggest-growing problems. Credit card fraud cost businesses billions of dollars each year, not to mention the stress and headache it causes for a victim of identity theft. Criminals find new ways every day to continue making this one of the biggest-growing crimes.

Protecting your identity is one of the most important things you can do. Never give your personal information to anyone who you are talking to that you don't know. Most companies will not ask for this type of information over the phone or will only ask for a portion such as the last four numbers of your social security number.

Before giving out any information, which can be used as identity or to obtain credit, confirm your call and who you are speaking with. Never give credit card information or checking account numbers over the phone, and do not leave this information lying around in your home.

Personal and credit information should be treated like it is top secret and should be protected at all cost. The three credit reporting agencies—being Experian, TransUnion, and Equifax—offer credit monitoring as well as credit reports for fees. You can obtain a copy of all three one time a year at anualcreditreport.com at no cost. You should keep a close watch on your credit. A new company called LifeLock offers the credit monitoring service for a fee but offers incentives to back their product. They can be found at www.lifelock.com.

Old checks, financial statements, or anything related to identity and finances should be shredded or burned once you are finished with them. Just throwing them away simply isn't enough anymore. Criminals will go through trash to obtain this type of information, so be safe and destroy it.

In this day and time, some criminals are very brave. Some who are not worried about being seen will actually come to your home and attempt to sell you something. Generally, there are two individuals. If you let them inside, while one is focusing your attention somewhere else, the other one will go through your purse, wallet, or drawers, taking information, personal checks, credits cards, or cash.

Never open your door for someone you don't know, especially if you are home alone and or live alone. Door-to-door sales were popular back in the '70's and '80s; however, with Internet sales, this is a thing of the past and very rarely is seen. Some businesses, such as vacuum cleaner sales, still do it some; but remember, you are still letting someone into your home you don't know. and you don't know the persons' criminal history.

Any door-to-door sales should have a door-to-door permit from your local business license office if it is required. Some city and county ordinances do not require it; however, most do. Be cautious of any service people who come to your door and want to come inside. Unless you are expecting them, they shouldn't need to come inside. If this is needed, most companies will make arrangements with you ahead of time.

On that note, I will say this. Just because they are with a company you are familiar with, it is not advisable to leave a service technician alone in your home unless you feel comfortable doing so. Again, this is someone you don't know, and if your credit card information or any other personal information is lying around, you don't know if they are the type to take it. Don't be too trusting.

Try to arrange the service time for when you are free to stay with them. Try and make others aware not to disturb you during this time, and try and stay free from distractions. Voice mail and answering machines come in handy during this time. Let them catch your calls while you are busy. Temptation is something not all individuals can pass up, so don't assist in providing the opportunity.

13

Various Theft Styles

A common type of theft nowadays is where someone will offer to seal your driveway or do some type of roofing work. They will ask for a sum of money up front, which could range anywhere from $500 to $2,500, and in some cases even more. You will pay them, and that will be the last time you see them or your money. Most of these individuals will focus on elderly couples or the elderly who live alone.

If approached by these persons at your home, do not open the door and ask them to leave a business card with you. Have them lay it on the porch or leave it by the door. Paying anyone you don't know up front for a job they haven't done is very risky. Always check with the Better Business Bureau and check for previous complaints or scam alerts. You can do this online at www.bbb.org.

While I am speaking to you about credit, fraud, and money, let me caution you about something known as a Ponzi scheme. This is where you invest large sums of money for the purchase of something that is then sold, and a return or percentage is paid to you. Anytime you are talking about money, it is always best to check around before jumping into something.

With a Ponzi scheme, the person taking in the money will collect money from one to pay to another. This is done until usually the money runs out and all you receive in exchange for your money is excuses and no return phone calls. Unless you can see in writing what is being done and can actually confirm the investment, I would suggest consulting an attorney or financial advisor first before doing anything.

These types of scams usually focus on persons who are wealthy and retired. Maybe even someone who is in business for themselves and has the extra cash, hoping to make good returns. The problem is you can lose thousands of dollars and have nothing to show for it. Even if the person is prosecuted, getting the money back you lost is not likely. Do a little investigating before you write any checks.

Internet and mail scams are on the rise. You will receive letters in the mail or in e-mail form, saying you have won a lottery or inherited money worth millions of dollars. You will receive a cashier's check in the mail for a certain amount usually around $2,500. All you have to do is cash the check, keep $500, and send the rest back to cover taxes and fees. If you have to *pay money to receive money*, this should be a clue.

My advice to you is shred the mail or delete the e-mail. This is a scam, and here is how it works. The cashier's check is no good (*fraudulent*), and once you cash it and send the $2,000, you have just started your problems. Your bank or whoever cashes the check will have it returned, and they will contact you for the money.

When you come to the police for help in your situation, you will find this crime is usually in relation to a Nigerian or European scam. Although they would like to help, their department will not send them to Nigeria or Europe to catch the bad guy. You will be responsible for paying back the $2,000 and will have to strike your misfortune as a lesson learned. *If it sounds too good to be true, it most likely is, so don't take a chance.*

If you are leaving to go out of town, stop your mail and paper service until you return. If for whatever reason you forget to do this, have a neighbor pick them up for you so they don't stack up. During interviews, I have had known thieves tell me this is how they picked some of their targets.

Criminals driving around see these types of things and realize no one is home. Contact your local law enforcement and let them know you are out of town so an extra patrol can be placed on your home. What this means is the officer assigned to your area during their shift will drive by and check your home more often than usual. Contact your local law enforcement nonemergency number to provide this information.

14

Car Safety

In this day and time, it amazes me the number of individuals who get out of their vehicle and leave it running, keys in the ignition, and the doors unlocked. Usually if there is a woman driving, her purse is lying on the seat as well. You should *never* leave your vehicle running for any reason, not even for a minute.

Statistics show that a car is stolen in the United States every twenty-three minutes. Unlike the vehicles from years ago, it is much harder to steal cars today due to added security features in the car itself. For this reason, many car thieves will hang out in common areas or ride around subdivisions looking for someone warming their car. All thieves have to do is jump in and drive off, which takes less than ten seconds. To avoid this, again never leave your keys in your car.

Technology today provides us with many wonderful inventions. If you are one of those who start your car to let it warm up, you can buy portable heaters, remote starters, or even battery-operated heaters to help achieve this goal. There are many available at different prices.

There are companies who offer location devices or GPS-type devices for vehicles. These can also be used on laptops, watercraft, ATVs, lawn or heavy equipment, as well as other properties, depending on the device. **LoJack** and **OnStar** are the two most common ones, but others are available. Shop around for prices and what best suits you.

It is a fact that unless your vehicle is recovered within an hour to two hours after it is stolen, it will not be in the condition you left it in once it is recovered. Depending on the type of vehicle, it may be stripped of certain parts, stripped altogether, or burned. The faster your vehicle is recovered, the better chances you have of getting it in one piece.

The other crime most common with vehicles is them getting broken into. This is commonly done by teenagers or gang members for amusement and money. Although you can't remove the stereo system from your car every time you get out, there are some steps you can take to reduce the chances of this happening to you.

Never leave anything of value visible in your car such as money, tools, weapons, GPS systems, jewelry, purchased gifts, and purses or wallets. Thieves will look inside your vehicle first to see if any of these items are visible. If you must leave items like these in your car, lock them in the trunk. Try and park your vehicle in a visible or well-lit area. This also works during the holidays while shopping.

15

Safety while Shopping

Since I have mentioned shopping, I will also share some other normal and holiday shopping tips for you. Shopping during the holidays is a hectic time. We all find ourselves in a hurry trying to get the best deals, and criminals see this as a great opportunity to commit crime on unsuspecting victims.

While shopping, pay close attention to who is around you and what is going on. Pay attention to individuals who seem to be wandering around but not really shopping. Their suspicious activity will make them stand out without even really trying to locate them. My suggestion is avoid those types of people; go in the opposite direction.

During your hectic time of looking for the right gift or even shopping for what is going to be supper tonight, don't move your attention away from your purse. While shopping, I find myself looking at women who walk away, leave their buggy unattended and their purse there for the taking. Never turn your back away from your purse or leave it unattended. Remember, it only takes a moment to snatch and conceal a wallet.

If possible, when you go shopping, take only what you need . Take cash, credit cards, or checkbook along with your shopping list and lock your purse in your trunk. Put these items on your person somewhere and take your purse out of the equation. If you must take it with you, keep your eyes on it like it is a child.

Another thing to consider is, there have been reports of women walking through a parking lot and criminals would drive close to them, grab the purse off their arm, or cut the strap and drive away with it. When walking back to your car, always keep your purse on the arm closest to the parked cars and not the traffic side.

I have also noticed during the holidays or even other times where someone will leave boxes for newly purchased large electronics at the end of the driveway. This tells criminals what you have in your home, and yes, they do look for these things. If you have these boxes, cut them up and place them in the trash can or into a large black trash bag. This will prevent others from seeing what you bought.

16

Safety while Driving

Okay, we have finished our shopping and now we are back in the car. Stressed out because we couldn't find what we were looking for, or after waiting in line for some time, someone cut in front of us and now we are running late. We need to hurry home and take care of kids, cook supper, or be somewhere in an hour. Stress level is high!

The absolute worst time to be driving a three-thousand-pound weapon is when you are mad, upset, or thinking about something. In this situation, your mind is not on driving your vehicle but rather on what upset you in the beginning. Take a moment before getting into your vehicle to allow yourself time to cool off. This will prevent you from focusing your anger on driving and taking it out on someone in front of you.

If someone does something such as cut you off, sit at a green light too long, or pull out in front of you, don't lay on your horn or use hand gestures to express your anger. Why? you may ask. Well, the very person you are expressing your anger at may be the very person you don't want to meet. You know nothing about this person, the frame of mind they are in, or to what extent they will go to get even with you.

Think before you act. The person you are expressing your anger at may be armed and in the frame of mind to use a weapon. Don't take the chance of placing yourself in a bad situation just to express your anger. To put it into plain English, *"Let it go!"* A simple horn toot will let someone know they are about to hit you or cut you off. Most of the time they will be alarmed and quickly move over.

If you encounter an aggressive driver, do not panic; instead, think. If someone comes up behind you riding your bumper, simply move over and let them pass. If you are moving over and they will not pass you, slow your vehicle until they do. Eventually, they may express their anger with a horn or may even use a hand sign, but they will pass and go on.

Keep in mind: if you have your family in the vehicle, their safety is your main concern. If you are on a two-lane road and the person is still behind you, pull off into a store or well-lit area so they may continue. If they pull off behind you, get back onto the road and call 911. Keep the dispatcher on the phone with you until the officer stops the vehicle or you lose sight of it.

Aggressive and reckless driving has been the cause of many serious injury crashes as well as fatal accidents. Anger behind the wheel is just as dangerous, if not more dangerous than a person with a loaded gun. If you find yourself *angry* behind the wheel of a vehicle, stop and get out of your vehicle. Get a drink, walk around, and allow yourself time to cool off before continuing on your journey. It may save your life.

Since we are talking about safety while driving, let me also mention cell phones. Most everyone these days has a cellphone and uses them on a regular basis. If you are one of these individuals, please be smart while using your phone. If you receive an important call, answer it, but tell the other party to hold on. Pull your car off the road safely and take the call. If it isn't important, let your voice mail catch it.

Cellphone-related accidents are very common. Some states have even banned the use of cell phones while driving. Either way, it is your responsibility to remain in control of your vehicle. Do not check e-mail, get on social networking sites, or play games on your phone while driving. *Absolutely* do not text and drive as this takes away your concentration while driving. *It can wait.*

One last thing I would like to mention about vehicles is your passengers. During the summertime, the inside of your vehicle heats up to very high temperatures, enough to cause death. Each year there are incidents of either children or pets being left in a hot vehicle, which usually results in death. *Please* take a minute before leaving your vehicle to make sure you have removed your children or pets. If going shopping, make arrangements to leave them with someone so leaving them in the vehicle is not an issue.

If you are someone who walks, rides a bike, or hikes for exercise, I always suggest doing it with a friend, never alone. If you are new to this form of exercise, talk to someone and find out the best place to do your activity. If you live in the city, you may have to drive somewhere to do your activity. So in this case, find out as much as you can about the area and check recent crime reports for that area.

If you are going alone, always make sure you tell someone your plans, where you are going, and the time you believe you should return. This way if something was to happen and you don't return, someone will know something is wrong and notify the proper authorities. Keep your cellphone with you so that you may be contacted.

17

Safety from Sexual Offenders

Whether doing exercise, going out shopping, or just running an errand, always remember to *stay alert and pay attention* to your surroundings. Whatever you are doing, try not to separate yourself from others or end up in a secluded area where no one is around. Many sexual predators and thugs look for these types of situations and use this as a hunting ground.

These predators also look for children and teenagers in this same situation, so talk with your children and make them aware. Always encourage them to remain in groups of friends and not to wander away alone. Safety is always best in groups, which is true not only for children but adults too.

If under any circumstance you find yourself becoming the victim of a robbery or carjacking, whether armed or unarmed, cooperate. If this person is armed with a gun, knife, or any other weapon, let them take whatever they want. Always remember, *property can be replaced; your life can't*. Be smart and think. Pay attention to clothing, hair, eyes, facial features, height, weight, scars, tattoos, or anything that you can use to help law enforcement identify your attacker.

The only time I would suggest resistance is in a life-or-death situation. If your life depends on it, *do not* give up. Use whatever means necessary to fight and escape. Be loud in the process by screaming, yelling, or whatever. Your attacker does not want attention drawn to his/her crime, so in some instances, they will get frightened and flee.

Smaller children are taught in school through the DARE program offered by many law enforcement agencies. This program covers drug awareness, violence, and safety about being approached by strangers. As a parent, it is always good to reiterate these things from time to time at home. It keeps it fresh in your child's mind.

One thing I always suggest is by playing a game I call what-if. You as a parent give your child certain scenarios that would place your child in a harmful situation. Allow your child to answer, and if they answer correctly praise them. If they give the wrong answer, reassure them it is okay and this is the time to make mistakes, not when they are actually in danger. Give them the answer and explain why.

Children are very naïve and gullible when they are young. Even as teenagers, when they seem to know the answer to everything in life, they know very little as to what is ahead of them. As a parent, we have a responsibility to talk with them about strangers, drugs, alcohol, sex, making bad choices, and hanging out with the wrong crowd. Don't wait for someone else to do it because then it may be too late.

Many children are abducted or kidnapped every year. Some are recovered with a happy ending, and some are not.

As I said, some children are naïve and believe anything someone tells them. Predators will use many lies to get their victims to quietly walk away with them without causing a scene. A situation like this makes it difficult as there are usually no witnesses or evidence at the scene.

A great way to prevent this is to create a word between you and your child. This code word would reassure your child that you are aware this person is picking them up. If the person trying to pick them up does not know the code word, then they should immediately go to another adult, police, school official, after-school caregiver, or a known adult.

If someone attempts to forcibly take your child, let them know it is okay to kick, scream, yell, or do whatever to draw attention to the attacker. Many of these individuals are known to flee if attention is drawn to them. Make sure if a code word is established, your child must keep this a secret. They should know this is your special word that they can't tell anyone. Make your code word something that only the two of you know.

You should always talk to your child about "good and bad" touches, making sure they know the difference. Most abusers will make threats or tell the child to keep it a secret. Let them know these are not secrets and Mommy, Daddy, or another adult should be told immediately if someone touches them in a bad way. Let your child know that no matter what this person has said, you will keep them safe.

18

Getting Involved in Ensuring Safety

Many people become complacent with everyday life and settle into a routine. Remember, it is very important to stay alert to what is happening around you as it could be the very thing that saves your life. We have all heard of the "gut feeling" and have all had it at some point in our lives. Truth is, your gut feeling will let you know when something isn't right, and most of the time it is correct.

If you are out somewhere or at home and see someone or something that doesn't look right, then chances are its not. Whatever it may be—a car, a person or strange activity—if it has caught your attention and seems strange, then you are probably right. If this happens, contact security or call 911 and let them look into it.

We live in a world now where everyone wants the world to be a better place. However, when it comes time to get involved, people back down and do nothing, hoping someone else will see it and take care of it. There are many crimes that occur that could be prevented just by someone calling 911, but the first step is picking up the phone.

Although it is great to have an eyewitness who is willing to testify for the court process, you do not have to give your name when calling 911 if you don't want to. Having said that, if you don't get involved and help put criminals where they belong, they will be back on the street to victimize someone else; however, the next victim could be you or someone you know or love.

Suspicious activity is just that, suspicious. Suspicious activity is that which is not normal and is unusual to the average person. Example would be if you have a house in a subdivision where activity happens all hours day and night. You have cars going in and out like a drive-through, and they are only there for five minutes or so and then leaves. It is very likely someone is dealing drugs, and it should be reported.

Another example would be Mr. Smith across the street is out of town. While looking out your window, you see someone climbing through a window at his house. It is very likely Mr. Smith's house is being broken into. These are common sense things that normal people see but do nothing about.

Remember, you live there and this is your neighborhood, which you and your family live in. The criminals living in your neighborhood will most likely not move unless you do something about it. Ignoring the problem will not make it go away, and by ignoring it, you risk the chance of being victimized by doing nothing. Reporting crime to the police only takes a phone call.

In this day and time with the Internet, you can now log on to some law enforcement agencies Web sites and file an anonymous complaint. This will then be investigated by police, without you being directly involved. *Never* take the law into your own hands unless you or someone else is in immediate danger; otherwise, call 911 or take the steps mentioned above.

Your local law enforcement needs and wants your help when you see suspicious activity. Law enforcement would much rather get your call, respond, and find out nothing is wrong as opposed to you not calling and something serious has happened. They are here to help but can't do it alone.

19

Ensuring Safety of the Children

I would like to mention one more thing for parents. As I mentioned earlier, the world has changed. There are more things out there that can harm our children and/or people that can take them away from us. No parent wants to bear the loss of a child or have to bury one. We as parents have to get more involved in our children's lives.

What I am talking about by getting more involved is this: know what your children are doing and who they are with. I have asked parents about going through a teenager's room, and they say, "No, I don't want to violate their privacy." You don't have to be a drill instructor parent, but you need to monitor your kids' activities and let them know you are watching.

Build a trusting relationship with your kids so they will talk to you and feel comfortable doing so. Being friends with them is okay, but don't forget to be a parent too. Talk to them about what is going on at school, at home, or just day-to-day activities. Let them know you are interested, and they are more likely to come to you with problems. Know who their friends are and invite them over. If your teenager doesn't want too, there is a reason.

Talk to other parents, the school counselor, or school resource officer about these kids and see if they are troublemakers. Monitor phone conversations and keep track of social networking site activities. Remember, some child predators will approach children on these sites, so know who they are talking to. *Set parental controls* that will alert you to their activity.

If your child has a cell phone, check with the carrier and see if it offers a GPS locator for parents. I know AT&T and Verizon wireless offer this service. It allows the parents to go online and see where your children are at and if they are where they said they would be. Remember, they are teenagers, and sometimes peer pressure is rough; we have all been there.

Depending on your child's age, go through their room on a regular basis, read letters, check text messages or e-mails, check drawers, closets and pockets. It is a fact that kids learn more at school about the "birds and the bees" than they do at home from the parents. If hanging with the wrong crowd, they will also learn about drugs, crime, and alcohol. Talk to your children before the wrong person does, or before it's too late. If your child has a sudden change in attitude, there is a reason; so as a parent, find out.

Believe me when I say there isn't a cop, nurse, doctor or anyone who wants to deliver the news to you that your child is dead. They are professionals, but they are also human. Teaching your children about these things starts at home, and being stern doesn't make you a bad parent. Tough love is just that, it's tough, but it is worth it in the end.

I hope in reading this book, you have taken in information to make you more alert to your surroundings. If you use some of the suggestions I have made while at home, at work, or during everyday activity, then you have taken the first step in reducing your chances of being victimized.

Remember, law enforcement can offer ways for you to make your home safer, but you as the home- or business owner have to do your part. Although they would love to be at every crime when it happens, they can't. This is why sharing this experience with you is a step toward reducing crime and helping to prevent people like you from becoming a victim. Stay alert and stay safe!

About the Author

Scott Lilly began his career in law enforcement in 1990, working for the Hall County Sheriff's Office in Gainesville, Georgia. Working his way up, in 1993 he was assigned to the Uniform Patrol Division where he responded to vast array of calls. These calls ranged from burglaries, domestic incidents, thefts, armed robberies, shootings, stabbings, and murders.

Each of these calls required the gathering of initial information to establish facts of crimes that occurred. This information came from evidence on the scene or speaking with victims, witnesses, or suspects.

Gathering this type of information provides experience in several different areas, especially when it comes to residential and commercial thefts. Methods of entry, time when these incidents occur, types of tools used to gain entry, and motivation for these crimes.

In 2003, Scott was promoted to the Criminal Investigations Division, starting as a narcotics agent. In 2005, Scott began working in the Property Crimes Division where he was assigned to investigate burglaries, thefts involving property and motor vehicles, as well as construction types of equipment. In 2010, Scott was assigned to the Crime Suppression Unit, made up of a group of patrol deputies and one investigator.

The focus of the Crime Suppression Unit was to aggressively patrol and focus on areas hardest hit with residential and commercial style burglaries, as well as thefts. The other focus was on known criminals who were on probation, parole, or out on bond for some type of theft-related charge. The unit was successful in reducing the number of burglaries in a year, by concentrating on these areas.

During his work as a property crimes investigator, Scott gained experience of certain criminals who operated in a single area or would spread out to multiple areas. In some incidents, Scott was able to establish an M/O (modus operandi), for some criminals using many of the same tactics in each of their crimes.

Having interviewed many suspects during his career, Scott was able to gain knowledge from these interviews. Knowledge about how entry was made, what the criminals looked for in choosing a particular target, or the things that prevented them from hitting a certain target. Scott is now sharing over twenty-one years of experience and knowledge of criminal activity to help reduce your chances of becoming a victim of crime.

CPSIA information can be obtained
at www.ICGtesting.com
Printed in the USA
LVOW12s0004160916
504815LV00013B/59/P